Martha Washington

by Candice Ransom

illustrations by Karen Ritz

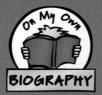

On My Own
BIOGRAPHY

M Millbrook Press/Minneapolis

With special thanks to Mary V. Thompson, research specialist at Mount Vernon

The portrait on page 46 appears with permission from the Washington-Custis-Lee Collection, Washington and Lee University, Lexington, Virginia.

Text copyright © 2003 by Candice Ransom
Illustrations copyright © 2003 by Karen Ritz

All rights reserved. International copyright secured. No part of this book may be reproduced, stored in a retrieval system, or transmitted in any form or by any means—electronic, mechanical, photocopying, recording, or otherwise—without the prior written permission of Lerner Publishing Group, Inc., except for the inclusion of brief quotations in an acknowledged review.

This book is available in two editions:
Library binding by Millbrook Press
    a division of Lerner Publishing Group, Inc.
Soft cover by First Avenue Editions,
    an imprint of Lerner Publishing Group, Inc.
241 First Avenue North
Minneapolis, MN 55401 USA

For reading levels and more information, look up this title at www.lernerbooks.com.

Library of Congress Cataloging-in-Publication Data

Ransom, Candice F., 1952–
    Martha Washington / by Candice Ransom ; illustrations by Karen Ritz.
        p.   cm. — (On my own biography)
    ISBN 978–0–87614–918–8 (lib. bdg. : alk. paper)
    ISBN 978–0–87614–107–6 (pbk. : alk. paper)
    ISBN 978–1–57505–711–8 (eBook)
    1. Washington, Martha, 1731–1802—Juvenile literature. 2. Presidents' spouses—United States—Biography—Juvenile literature. I. Ritz, Karen. II. Title. III. Series.
E312.19.W34 R36 2003
973.4'1'092—dc21   2002001536

Manufactured in the United States of America
5-45958-3138-5/15/2018

For Chris, the peacemaker — C. R.

Williamsburg, Virginia
1746–1759

Martha Dandridge hoped someone
would ask her to dance.
The Assembly Ball
was an important event.
Young men would see she was
a proper young lady.

She knew how to greet
the royal governor.
She knew how to dance
with her toe pointed.
She could even play the spinet and sing.
She would make someone
a fine wife someday.

A gentlemen asked Martha to dance.

He was Daniel Parke Custis.

Daniel was one of the richest landowners
in the British colony of Virginia.

And he was kind and gentle.

Many women wanted to marry him.

After the ball,

Daniel often visited Martha at her home.

Martha slowly fell in love with him.

In 1749, they were married.

Martha went to live in Daniel's
big white house on his tobacco plantation.

They had four children there.

Martha lived like a lady.

She had fine clothes and a beautiful home.

And like most rich people,
she and Daniel owned many slaves.

Martha hoped her life would always
be the same.

But sadness came to her.

Two of her children became sick and died.

Later Daniel died, too.

He left Martha his tobacco plantation
and his large home.

She ran the plantation as well as any man.

But she was lonely.

Martha was only 26 years old,
too young to be a widow.

One night she met a tall, quiet gentleman
at a dinner party.

His name was George Washington.

Colonel Washington was a hero.

He had fought bravely in the British army
in a war against the French and the Indians.

Martha liked George Washington.
And she was ready for a new life.
When he asked her to marry him,
she said yes.

Mount Vernon, Virginia

1759

Martha stepped down from the coach.
She looked at the big house
on the banks of the Potomac River.

George lifted her children,
Jacky and Patsy, from the coach.
He had brought them to his home.
Martha hoped she and the children
would be happy here.

Martha was now the mistress
of Mount Vernon.
Every morning,
she put on a white cotton dress.
She planned meals with the cook.
She made sure the ironing
was done properly.
She worked in the garden.

Running Mount Vernon was a big job.
But Martha liked making everything
perfect for George and the children.
George was often out managing his farm.
Sometimes he went to Williamsburg,
the capital of Virginia.
There he worked as a lawmaker
for the British colony.
Whenever he returned home,
Martha was sure to be ready.
She would wear a pretty silk gown.
White powder frosted her hair.
Martha was happy with her life
as Mrs. Washington.

Mount Vernon, Virginia
1773

Martha sipped from her cup.

She wrinkled her nose.

Tea made from goldenrod tasted strange.

Martha liked British tea much better.

But the Washingtons had stopped

buying tea from Great Britain.

Britain made the colonists pay a tax on tea.

Other goods had also been taxed.

14

But the colonists argued that the taxes
were unfair.

The king agreed to take away most taxes.

But he refused to take away the tax on tea.

To show their anger, George and other
colonists stopped buying British tea.

Martha had worries of her own.

Patsy was ill.

And Jacky had decided to quit school
and get married.

That summer, Patsy died.

Martha was so sad,

she did not go to Jacky's wedding.

But slowly she became used to
the changes at home.
Many guests visited Mount Vernon.
They often argued about Great Britain.
The king still tried to control the colonies.
And the colonists were angrier than ever.
Martha wondered what would happen next.

Mount Vernon, Virginia
1774

Martha listened to Patrick Henry's
strong words against the British.
Mr. Henry and Edmund Pendleton were
spending the night at Mount Vernon.
They would ride with George to Philadelphia,
Pennsylvania, for an important meeting.

They were joining men from all over
the colonies for the Continental Congress.
The Congress's job was to fight
for the rights of the colonies.
"I hope you will all stand firm,"
Martha told her guests.
"I know George will."

Two months later,

George returned home.

He told Martha that the colonies

had decided to unite against Britain.

They would stop buying all British goods.

In May 1775, George left once more

for Philadelphia.

Martha received a letter from him in June.

America was at war with Britain.

And the colonists wanted George to lead

the Continental Army.

Martha wished George could come home.

She missed him terribly.

But she understood that the colonies

needed him.

That winter, Martha received
an important request.
George wanted her to come
to his army camp for Christmas.
Martha had never been so far from home.
Cambridge, Massachusetts,
was 600 miles away!
British soldiers might try to capture
the wife of George Washington.
But nothing would keep her from George.

Martha packed some things
and tried not to think about the dangers.
The ride to Cambridge took weeks.
Her coach bounced over rough roads.
She passed fields, woods,
and strange towns.
On December 11, her driver stopped
in front of a yellow house.
This was General Washington's
headquarters.

Martha got to work right away.

She visited soldiers, cooked, and cleaned.

She gave soldiers hams, jellies,

and dried fruits from Mount Vernon.

She was cheerful even when cannons

fired in the distance.

She tried to be cheerful for George, too.

He was worried.

His men needed supplies.

How could they win a war

without food or guns?

Martha hoped George's problems

would be solved soon.

Valley Forge, Pennsylvania
1778

Snow lay in deep drifts.
Smoke curled from the roofs
of hundreds of wooden huts.
A guard saluted Martha
as her sleigh drove by.
His feet were in his hat
because he had no shoes.
He wore an old ragged blanket
instead of a warm coat.
Many of the soldiers were suffering
this way.

For the last three winters,
George had sent for Martha.
Every winter, she went.
The camps were always
in different places.
And it was always cold.

Martha had become used
to hardship.
But this winter was the worst.
The army was starving and freezing.
British troops had destroyed
the army's supplies.
Wagons could not bring more supplies
over snowy, muddy roads.

The ladies living in nearby towns
were surprised by Mrs. Washington.
They thought the general's wife would
hold grand parties.
They expected her to wear
beautiful gowns.
Instead, Martha cared for soldiers
and wore a plain brown dress.

With a basket over her arm,
Martha visited the soldiers' huts.
She brought them food and medicine
from Mount Vernon.
She patched shirts
and knitted stockings.

Martha did not complain
about the cold.
She did not mind living
in a cramped house.
She would do anything to help
her husband win the war.

Mount Vernon, Virginia
1783

Pine wreaths decorated the house.

Brass lanterns gleamed.

Freshly baked pies and cakes

filled pantry shelves.

It was Christmas Eve.

Martha wondered if George

would make it home.

The war was finally over.

He was an American hero.

And a new nation was born.

It was called the United States of America.

Martha could hardly wait to see George.

But a sadness hung over her.

Jacky had lost his life during the war,

and she still missed him.

Two of Jacky's children

lived with her.

Martha had adopted Little Washington

and Nelly after Jacky died.

Suddenly there was a shout outside.

It was George, riding to the house.

Martha ran to greet him.

With George home,

her family would be happy again.

Martha was busier than ever.

Many people visited Mount Vernon.

Martha made each guest feel at home.

She worked from dawn till past dark.

Bedrooms were cleaned and ready.

Hearty breakfasts and huge dinners
were planned.

Then Martha's life changed again.

In 1789, George was elected to be
the first president of the United States.
He would live and work in New York City,
the nation's capital.
Martha did not want to leave home.
But she would not be parted
from her husband.
And the nation needed George.

New York

1789

Boom! Ka-boom!

Thirteen guns blasted the air.

Crowds cheered, and church bells rang.

George said the welcome

was just for Martha!

The Washingtons drove to their

new home on Cherry Street.

That very night,

George held an important dinner.

Martha did not like what she saw.

Conversation was stiff and dull.

Servants made mistakes.

This would never do.

Martha knew that the president's house

should be more than a home.

It should be an important

meeting place, too.

That Friday, Martha hosted a party.
Important guests drank tea and ate cake.
Martha made sure there was plenty
to talk about.
Everyone felt welcomed.
After that, Martha hosted a party
every Friday night.
And she kept the president's house
running smoothly.

Martha's household duties kept her busy.
But she always made time for George.
When he was ill,
she took care of him.
When he had a problem to discuss,
she listened.

In 1790, the Washingtons moved
to Philadelphia.
Presidents would live there until the new
capital was built along the Potomac River.
Martha had many friends in Philadelphia.
Still, she missed Mount Vernon.
After four years,
she was ready to go home.
But George was elected to a second term.
Another four years!
Martha worried about George.
He worked late every night.
His hair had turned white.
He had trouble hearing and seeing.
When he was asked to stay
for a third term, George said no.

He was tired.
It was time for someone else
to lead the country.

In March 1797,
the Washingtons left
for Mount Vernon.
They traveled with 97 boxes, 14 trunks,
George's dog, and Martha's parrot.

As she stepped from the carriage,
Martha gazed at Mount Vernon.
It felt wonderful to be home at last.
And if felt good to know she had served
her country well.

Artist John Wollaston made this painting of Martha when she was still married to Daniel Parke Custis.

Afterword

In December 1799, George became ill with a sore throat and high fever. He died a few days later on December 14.

After his death, Martha closed their bedroom and moved to a small, plain room on the third floor of Mount Vernon. Her only furnishings were a bed, two chairs, and a stove. She spent her last years quietly, gardening and reading.

Sometime before her own death, Martha burned all the letters between her and George. Two letters managed to survive, both from George. These letters were found in a desk by Martha's granddaughter.

Martha Washington died at Mount Vernon on May 22, 1802. She is buried next to George. Martha Washington is remembered for being kind, gracious, and strong. America's first First Lady set an example for all the presidents' wives who followed her.

Important Dates

1731—Martha Washington is born on June 2 near Williamsburg, Virginia.

1749—Martha marries Daniel Parke Custis.

1757—Daniel dies.

1759—Martha marries George Washington on January 6.

1773—Great Britain passes the Tea Act; Patsy dies in June.

1774—The First Continental Congress meets in Philadelphia on September 4.

1775—George is chosen to lead the Continental Army; Martha makes her first trip to George's winter camp.

1781—Jacky dies during the war; Martha adopts Nelly and Little Washington.

1783—The Revolutionary War ends.

1789—George Washington is elected president; the Washingtons move to New York City.

1790—The Washingtons move to Philadelphia.

1797—The Washingtons return to Mount Vernon in March.

1799—George dies on December 14.

1802—Martha Washington dies on May 22.